Half

Harvest Cookbook

Half Cooked Harvest Cookbook: no-nonsense, quick and delicious daily recipes for the whole family

The information in the following pages is broadly considered a truthful and accurate account of facts and as such, any inattention, use, or misuse of the information in question by the reader will render any resulting actions solely under their purview. There are no scenarios in which the publisher or the original author of this work can be in any fashion deemed liable for any hardship or damages that may befall them after undertaking information described herein.

Additionally, the information in the following pages is intended only for informational purposes and should thus be thought of as universal. As befitting its nature, it is presented without assurance regarding its prolonged validity or interim quality. Trademarks that are mentioned are done without written consent and can in no way be considered an endorsement from the trademark holder.

TABLE OF CONTENTS

BREAKFAST

Cheesy Ham Breakfast Casserole

Preparation Time: 10 minutes

Cooking Time: 10 minutes

Servings: 4

Ingredients

- 8 eggs
- 1 cup milk
- salt and pepper to taste
- 2 cups diced ham
- 1 cup shredded cheddar cheese

Directions

1. Preheat oven to 350 degrees F (175 degrees C). Beat eggs in a large bowl, making sure that they are mixed very well and have a 'frothy' top. Add the milk, salt and pepper. Mix well. Stir in ham, then add cheese pieces and stir well.
2. Pour mixture into a well-greased 4-quart casserole dish and bake in the preheated oven for 50 to 60 minutes or until top is lightly browned.

Nutrition: 386 Calories 14g Fat 15g Protein 4g Carbs

Blue Cheese Scrambled Eggs

Preparation Time: 10 minutes

Cooking Time: 5 minutes

Servings: 3

Ingredients

- 3 large eggs
- 1/4 cup 1% milk
- 1 tsp dried parsley
- 1/2 tsp dried thyme
- 1 scant tbsp of finely crumpled blue cheese

Directions:

1. Preheat a 9" nonstick skillet over low heat. Combine all ingredients except the blue cheese in a mixing bowl. Wisk with a fork for about 10-15 seconds.
2. Once skillet is heated, spray of the non-stick canola cooking spray to the skillet. Pour egg mixture into pan and constantly scrambling.
3. When almost done to you desired level of doneness, remove pan from heat and adjust the seasonings to your taste.
4. Sprinkle the blue cheese evenly over the eggs and return the pan to heat until the cheese begins to melt.

Nutrition: 180 Calories 12g Fat 13g Protein 3.5g Carbs

Salsa Scrambled Eggs

Preparation Time: 10 minutes

Cooking Time: 10 minutes

Servings: 4

Ingredients

- 1 tablespoon butter
- 1/4 cup chopped onion
- 4 eggs, beaten
- 1/4 cup Salsa
- 2 tablespoons crumbled feta cheese

Directions

1. Melt butter in a skillet over medium heat. Sauté onions until translucent. Pour in eggs. Cook, stirring occasionally to scramble. When eggs appear almost done, stir in salsa and feta cheese, and season with salt and pepper. Cook until cheese is melted.

Nutrition: 113 Calories 7g Fat 8g Protein 2.5g Carbs

Mediterranean Style Scrambled Eggs

Preparation Time: 10 minutes

Cooking Time: 5 minutes

Servings: 4

Ingredients

- 4 eggs
- 3 chopped cherry tomatoes
- 1/4 cup of feta cheese
- 3 tbsp chopped cilantro
- 1/4 cup of chopped scallions

Directions:

1. Scramble eggs, when it starts to bubble add in other ingredients and continue until completely scrambled.

Nutrition: 352 Calories 25g Fat 26g Protein 4g Carbs

Spinach and Cream Cheese Omelet

Preparation Time: 10 minutes

Cooking Time: 5 minutes

Servings: 2

Ingredients

- 2 oz cream cheese
- 2 large eggs
- 1/4 cup chopped fresh spinach
- 1/4 tsp sesame seed oil

Directions:

1. In a bowl, mix together cream cheese and spinach. In a separate bowl, beat 2 eggs.
2. Brush sesame seed oil on the bottom of a frying pan. Preheat pan on medium heat, pour in eggs. Cook until able to flip egg. Spread cream cheese mixture onto cooked side of egg.
3. Wait 30 seconds to ensure the other side of the egg is cooked, fold in half, and wait 1 minute to melt cream cheese mixture. Remove from heat, serve.

Nutrition: 360 Calories 31g Fat 17g Protein 3g Carbs

skinny
fork

Swedish Scrambled eggs

Preparation Time: 5 minutes

Cooking Time: 10 minutes

Servings: 4

Ingredients:

- 8 eggs
- 2 tablespoons fresh dill, finely chopped or 3 teaspoons dried dill
- Salt to taste
- Pepper to taste
- 8 ounces cream cheese, chopped into small cubes
- ¼ teaspoon garlic powder
- Nonstick cooking spray

Directions:

1. Add eggs into a container and whisk until pale and foamy. Add rest of the ingredients and stir until well combined. Place a skillet over high heat. Spray cooking spray over it. Add the egg combination into the pot. Lower heat to medium and stir. Scramble and cook the eggs until the consistency you desire is achieved.

Nutrition: Calories: 210 Fat: 8.5g Fiber: 2.5g Carbs: 27g Protein: 4g

Spinach Tomato Frittata

Preparation Time: 10 minutes

Cooking Time: 15-25 minutes

Servings: 8

Ingredients:

- 6 eggs
- 1/3 cup grated Parmesan cheese
- 1/2 tsp. garlic powder
- 1/2 tsp. dried basil
- 1/4 tsp. salt
- 1/4 tsp. black pepper
- 1/8 tsp. ground nutmeg
- 2 tsp. olive oil
- 6 cups fresh spinach
- 6 cherry tomatoes, quartered

Directions:

1. In a small bowl, add the eggs, Parmesan cheese, garlic powder, basil, salt, black pepper and nutmeg. Whisk until well combined. In a skillet over medium heat, add the olive oil. When the oil is hot, add the spinach. Saute the spinach for 3 minutes.

2. Reduce the heat to low. Spread the spinach evenly in the skillet. Sprinkle the tomatoes over the spinach. Pour the eggs over the spinach but do not stir. Place a lid on the skillet. When the bottom of the frittata is set, lift the edges to allow the uncooked egg to run underneath. Cook for 12 minutes or until the frittata is set in the center and the bottom browned. Remove the skillet from the heat and serve.

Nutrition: Calories: 298 Fat: 10.5g Fiber: 3.6g Carbs: 29.9g Protein: 10g

Breakfast Sausage Casserole

Preparation Time: 10 Minutes

Cooking Time: 1 hour

Servings: 6

Ingredients:

- 1 lb. breakfast sausage
- 3 cups shredded potatoes, drained and pressed
- 1/4 cup salted butter, melted
- 12 ounces Gruyere cheese, shredded
- 1/2 cup onion, shredded
- 16-ounce Ricotta cheese
- 6 jumbo eggs

Directions:

1. Preheat the oven to 375 degrees F. Lightly grease a 9x13 inch casserole dish. Over medium high heat cooks the sausage & turn it often until evenly browned. Drain and crumble the sausage then set aside. Stir the butter & the potatoes together and line the bottom of the baking dish with this mixture. Mix the sausage, cheeses, onion and eggs in a separate bowl and pour this over the potato mixture. Bake for 1 hour until a toothpick inserted into

the casserole comes out clean. Let it cool down for 20-30 min. before serving.

Nutrition: Calories: 223.6 kcal Fat: 15.4 g Carbs: 7.6 g Sodium: 460.9 mg Protein: 13.2 g

APPETIZER AND SIDES

Kale Chips

Preparation Time: 5 minutes

Cooking Time: 15-20 minutes

Servings: 4-5

Ingredients:

- ¼ cup vegetable broth
- 1 tablespoon nutritional yeast
- ½ teaspoon garlic powder
- ½ teaspoon onion powder
- 6 ounces kale, stemmed and cut into 2- to 3-inch pieces

Directions:

1. Preheat the oven to 300°F. Line a baking sheet with parchment paper. In a small bowl, mix the broth, nutritional yeast, garlic powder, and onion powder. Put the kale in a large bowl. Pour the broth and seasonings over the kale, and toss well to coat thoroughly. Place the kale pieces on the baking sheet in an even layer. Bake for

20 minutes, or until crispy, turning the kale halfway through.

Nutrition: Calories: 120 Fat: 7.6g Fiber: 4.5g Carbs: 20.4g Protein: 5g

Roasted Tandoori Cauliflower

Preparation Time: 5 minutes

Cooking Time: 15-20 minutes

Servings: 8

Ingredients:

- ½ cup almond butter
- 4 teaspoons tandoori paste
- 2 teaspoons water
- 1 head cauliflower, cut into 1-inch florets
- 2 tablespoons canola oil
- ½ lemon

Directions:

1. Preheat the oven to 450°F. In a large bowl, stir together the almond butter, tandoori paste, and water. Add the cauliflower and toss to coat. On a roasting pan, add the oil to cover the bottom and spread the cauliflower on the pan. Cook for 10-15 minutes until the cauliflower is tender. Turn the oven to broil on high and cook for 2-3 minutes, until the tops begin to brown. Squeeze the lemon over the cauliflower before serving.

Nutrition: Calories: 189 Fat: 10.5g Fiber: 6g Carbs:29.2g Protein: 5.5 g

Pineapple Fried Rice

Preparation Time: 15 minutes

Cooking Time: 10-15 minutes

Servings: 8

Ingredients:

- Sauce
- ¼ cup low-sodium soy sauce
- 2 tablespoons toasted sesame oil
- 1 tablespoon brown sugar
- 2 garlic cloves, minced
- 1 teaspoon powdered ginger
- ¼ teaspoon pepper
- 2 tablespoons canola oil
- 1 medium onion, diced
- 2 carrots, peeled and grated
- ½ cup frozen corn
- ½ cup frozen peas
- 3 cups cooked basmati rice (preferably refrigerated overnight)
- 2 cups diced fresh pineapple
- 2 green onions, sliced diagonally

Directions:

1. In a small bowl, whisk together soy sauce, sesame oil, brown sugar, garlic, ginger, and pepper. Set aside. In a large pan over medium heat, warm the oil. Add the onions and cook about 3-4 minutes, stirring often, until they become translucent. Add the carrots, corn, and peas to the pan, cooking about 3-4 minutes, until the vegetables are tender. Stir in the cooked rice, pineapple, green onions, and soy sauce mixture, stirring constantly. Cook about 4 minutes, until heated through.
2. Note: Fresh cooked rice works here as well, but pre-cooking and refrigerating the rice a day ahead gives you the texture most desired in a fried rice dish. To ensure food safety, be sure to spread the rice in a shallow layer before refrigerating, so it cools quickly.

Nutrition: Calories: 298 Fat: 10.6g Fiber: 9g Carbs: 30 g Protein: 5g

Baked French Fries

Preparation Time: 10 minutes

Cooking Time: 40 minutes

Servings: 8

Ingredients:

- 1 tbsp. canola oil
- 6 Russet potatoes, cut into fries
- 1 tsp. sugar
- 3 tbsp. garlic-flavored olive oil
- 1 teaspoon garlic powder, or more to taste
- Salt and pepper to taste
- ½ tsp. cayenne pepper
- ½ tsp. chili powder
- ¼ cup parmesan cheese

Directions:

1. Preheat the oven to 425 degrees. Coat a baking sheet with non-stick spray. Dust the potatoes with sugar and let sit for 30 minutes. Drain any liquid. Place the potatoes, olive oil, garlic powder, salt, pepper, cayenne pepper, and chili powder in a bag and shake until the potatoes are coated. Transfer the potato to the baking sheet. Sprinkle the potatoes with parmesan cheese. Bake for 20 minutes. Turn the fries over and bake for another 20 minutes.

Nutrition: Calories: 450 Fat: 22.5g Fiber: 5.5g Carbs: 42.2g Protein: 7g

Asian Marinated Mushrooms

Preparation Time: 5 minutes

Cooking Time: 8 hrs

Servings: 10

Ingredients:

- ¼ cup rice vinegar
- ½ cup brown sugar
- ½ teaspoon chili powder
- 1 cup soy sauce
- 1 cup water
- 2 pounds mushrooms

Directions:

1. Throw all the ingredients into your crock pot and mix. Secure the lid, switch your slow cooker to low setting and cook for about eight hours. Let cool in the pot before you serve.

Nutrition: Calories: 150 Fat: 8g Fiber: 2.5g Carbs: 16.2g Protein: 4g

LUNCH

Fish Taco Bowl

Preparation Time: 10 Minutes

Cooking Time: 15 Minutes

Servings: 2

Ingredients:

- 2 (5-ounce) tilapia fillets
- One tablespoon olive oil
- Four teaspoons Tajin seasoning salt, divided
- 2 cups pre-sliced coleslaw cabbage mix
- One tablespoon avocado mayo
- 1 tsp. hot sauce
- One avocado, mashed
- Pink Himalayan salt
- Freshly ground black pepper

Directions:

1. Preheat the oven to 425 F. The baking sheet must be lined with a baking mat.

2. Rub the tilapia with the olive oil, and then coat it with Tajín seasoning salt with two teaspoons.
3. Place the fish in the prepared pan.
4. Let the tilapia bake for 15 minutes, or until the fish is opaque when you pierce it with a fork.
5. Meanwhile, in a medium bowl, gently mix to combine the coleslaw and the mayo sauce.
6. You don't want the cabbage super wet, just enough to dress it.
7. Add the mashed avocado and the remaining two teaspoons of Tajín seasoning salt to the coleslaw, and season with pink Himalayan salt and pepper.
8. Divide the salad between two bowls.
9. Shred fish into tiny pieces, and add it to the bowls.
10. Top the fish with a drizzle of mayo sauce and serve.

Nutrition: Calories: 231 Fat: 12.1g Fiber: 10.3g Carbohydrates:2.1 g Protein: 17.3g

Cajun Lobster Tails

Preparation Time: 10 Minutes

Cooking Time: 20 Minutes

Servings: 4

Ingredients:

- 1 lb. of peeled and deveined raw Lobster
- 1 Cup of almond flour
- 1 tbsp. of pepper
- 1 tbsp. of salt
- 1 tsp. of cayenne pepper
- 1 tsp. of cumin
- 1 tsp. of garlic powder
- 1 tbsp. of paprika
- 1 tbsp. of onion powder

Directions:

1. Preheat your fryer to a temperature of 390° F. Peel the lobster and devein it.
2. Dip the lobster into the heavy cream.
3. Dredge the lobster into the mixture of the almond flour. Shake off any excess flour.
4. Put the lobster in the fryer and cook for about 15 minutes and the temperature to 200° C/400° F.
5. You can check your appetizer after about 6 minutes, and you can flip the lobster if needed. Serve and enjoy your lobsters!

Nutrition: Calories: 321 Fat: 14.1g Fiber: 12.1g Carbohydrates: 3.2g Protein: 8.5g

Spicy Shrimp Skewers

Preparation Time: 5 Minutes

Cooking Time: 9 Minutes

Servings: 4

Ingredients:

- 2 tbsp. Paprika
- 1/2 tbsp. Onion powder
- 1/2 tbsp. dried thyme, crushed
- 1-pound shrimp, peeled and deveined
- 2 tbsp. Olive oil
- 1/2 tbsp. Red chili powder
- 1/2 tbsp. Garlic powder
- 1/2 tbsp. dried oregano, crushed
- Two zucchinis, cut into 1/2-inch cubes

Directions:

1. Preheat the grill to medium-high heat.
2. In a bowl, mix spices and dried herbs.
3. In a large bowl, add shrimp, zucchini, oil, and seasoning and toss to coat well.
4. Thread shrimp and zucchini onto pre-soaked skewers.
5. Grill the skewers for about 6-8 minutes, flipping occasionally. Serve hot.

Nutrition: Calories: 261 Fat: 9.4g Fiber: 10.1g Carbohydrates:3.2 g Protein: 4.1g

Crack Slaw

Preparation Time: 5 Minutes

Cooking Time: 35 Minutes

Servings: 4

Ingredients:

- Two tablespoons butter, ghee, or coconut oil
- 1-pound ground pork or sausage
- One small head of green cabbage, shredded
- Two tablespoons liquid or coconut aminos
- One tablespoon fish sauce
- One tablespoon coconut vinegar or apple cider vinegar
- One teaspoon garlic powder
- One teaspoon onion powder
- ¼ teaspoon ground ginger
- Pinch red pepper flakes
- Pinch sea salt
- Pinch freshly ground black pepper
- One scallion, chopped

Directions:

1. In a large skillet over medium heat, melt the butter or heat the oil and add the ground pork or sausage. Cook, stirring, until browned, 5 to 7 minutes.

2. Add the shredded cabbage and mix to combine. Add the aminos, fish sauce, vinegar, garlic powder, onion powder, ginger, and red pepper flakes and mix well.
3. Simmer on low for 20 to 30 minutes, occasionally stirring, until the cabbage is cooked down and tender.
4. Season with salt and pepper and top with the chopped scallion.
5. Serve immediately or store in the refrigerator for up to 1 week.

Nutrition: Calories: 356 Total Fat: 24g Protein: 24g Total Carbs: 11g

Pork Fried Cauliflower Rice

Preparation Time: 10 Minutes

Cooking Time: 20 Minutes

Servings: 4

Ingredients:

- 1-pound ground pork
- Sea salt
- Freshly ground black pepper
- Three tablespoons toasted sesame oil
- 3 cups thinly sliced cabbage
- 1 cup chopped broccoli
- One red bell pepper, cored and chopped
- One garlic clove, minced
- 1½ cups riced cauliflower
- One tablespoon sriracha
- Two tablespoons liquid aminos or tamari
- One teaspoon rice wine vinegar
- One teaspoon sesame seed, for garnish

Directions:

1. Heat a medium skillet over medium-high heat. Put the pork and sprinkle generously with salt and pepper.

Cook, frequently stirring, until browned, about 10 minutes. Take away the meat from the skillet.

2. Lessen the heat to medium and add the sesame oil to the skillet and cabbage, broccoli, bell pepper, riced cauliflower, and garlic. Cook for about 5 minutes until somewhat softened, then add the sriracha, liquid aminos, and vinegar and mix well.
3. Put the browned pork back in the skillet. Simmer together for around 5 minutes more until the cabbage is tender.
4. Season with salt and pepper, then garnish with the sesame seeds and serve right away.

Nutrition: Calories: 460 Total Fat: 36g Protein: 23g Total Carbs: 11g

DINNER

Vegetarian Portobello Pot Roast

Preparation Time: 10 minutes

Cooking Time: 1 hour and 10 minutes

Servings: 6-8

Ingredients:

- 1 pound portobello mushrooms, cut into two inch pieces
- 2 large carrots, peeled and diced
- 3 large parsnips, diced large
- 1 rib of celery, chopped
- 1 cup frozen pearl onions
- 4 cloves garlic, peeled and minced
- 3 sprigs fresh thyme
- 3 cups vegetable stock, divided
- 1/2 cup dry red wine
- 3 tbsp. tomato paste
- 2 tbsp. Vegetarian Worcestershire sauce
- 2 tbsp. cornstarch
- Kosher salt and freshly-cracked black pepper

- Egg noodles with butter, optional side

Directions:

1. Add mushrooms, carrots, parsnips, celery, onions, garlic, thyme, 2 1/2 cups vegetable stock, wine and Worcestershire to the inner pan of the rice cooker; gently toss to combine. Lock the lid in place and mixed key for a total of one hour.
2. Whisk together the remaining 1/2 cup vegetable stock and cornstarch until well-combined. Add to the pot roast and gently toss to combine. Continue on the mixed key for an additional 5 minutes, until the sauce thickens. Serve hot with buttered egg noodles.

Nutrition: Calories 165 Fat 0.6g Carbohydrates 32.8g Dietary Fiber 7.5g Protein 4.5g

Hawaiian Fried Rice

Preparation Time: 10 minutes

Cooking Time: 50 minutes

Servings: 6

Ingredients:

- 2 tsp. sesame oil
- 1/2 tsp. garlic powder
- 1 small onion, diced
- 1 red bell pepper, diced
- 2 cups uncured ham, cooked and diced into 1/2 inch cubes
- 3 eggs
- 1 1/2 cups brown rice, uncooked and rinsed
- 2 cups water
- 2 tbsp. soy sauce
- 1 cup pineapple, diced
- 1 scallion, sliced thin, for garnish

Directions:

1. Add the sesame oil to the inner pan and select the mixed key for five minutes. Heat oil for 2 minutes, then add the onion and red pepper to sauté for the remaining 3 minutes. Stir and sauté for 5 additional minutes or until

softened. Add the ham to the rice cooker and sauté for 5 minutes.

2. Put eggs in a bowl and beat until well-combined. Push the ham mixture to one side and add the eggs and scramble until firm and cooked through. Add remaining ingredients, stir to combine, lock the lid in place, and set to mixed key for 25 minutes. Leave Hawaiian Fried Rice on keep warm for 10 minutes. Serve rice into bowls and garnish with scallion.

Nutrition: Calories 245 Dietary Fiber 2.6g Fat 7.1g Carbohydrates 43.8g Protein 15.9g

General Tso's Chicken

Preparation Time: 10 minutes

Cooking Time: 45 minutes

Servings: 2-4

Ingredients:

- 3 garlic cloves, minced
- 1 tsp. fresh ginger, roughly chopped
- 1 tbsp. grapeseed oil
- 10 dried Chinese red chili
- 5 boneless skinless chicken thighs
- 1 stalk green onion, green part finely chopped for garnish, white part cut into 1.5-inch pieces
- 1 tbsp. honey
- 8-10 pieces of bibb lettuce or romaine
- General Tso's Sauce
- 1/4 cup dark soy sauce
- 2 tbsp. Shaoxing rice wine
- 2 tbsp. distilled white vinegar
- 1/3 cup sugar or sugar substitute
- 1 tsp. sesame oil
- Thickening Agent
- 2 tbsp. cornstarch

- 2 tbsp. water

Directions:

1. Whisk together the General Tso's Sauce ingredients in a glass mixing bowl until well-combined and set aside. Add grapeseed oil to the rice cooker and add 5 minutes to the mixed key. Add garlic and ginger after 2 minutes. Sauté until translucent and softened for about 3 minutes. Add dried Chinese red chili, the whites of the green onions. Cook for 3 minutes until fragrant. Add sauce and chicken thighs to the inner pan. Close the lid and mixed key for 25 minutes.
2. Remove the chicken from the inner pan and shred with a fork. Remove the Chinese red chili. Add honey and bring the sauce back to a boil on a mixed key. Mix the cornstarch and water for the thickening agent in a small mixing bowl. Fold into the sauce one third at a time until desired thickness. Fold shredded chicken into the sauce and replace the lid on and keep warm for 5 minutes.
3. Assemble lettuce leaves on a plate. Spoon in the desired amount of General Tso's Chicken and garnish with green onion to serve.

Nutrition: Calories 187 Fat 8g Carbohydrates 6.7g Dietary Fiber 0.2g Protein 22.6g

Super-Easy Spanish Paella

Preparation Time: 10 minutes

Cooking Time: 40 minutes

Servings: 6

Ingredients:

- 2 tbsp. olive oil, divided
- 1 yellow onion, diced
- 1 red bell pepper, diced
- 1 green bell pepper, diced
- 2 cloves garlic, minced
- 2 tsp. smoked paprika
- 2 tsp. dried oregano
- 1 pinch saffron
- 3/4 tsp. sea salt
- 1/2 tsp. crushed red pepper flakes
- Coarse ground black pepper
- 1 bay leaf
- 1 (15 oz.) can diced tomatoes
- 3 cups low-sodium vegetable or chicken broth
- 11/2 cups brown rice
- 3 boneless skinless chicken thighs, cut into 1-inch pieces
- 12 large shrimp or tiger prawns, deveined and peeled

- 1/4 cup chorizo
- 1/2 cup frozen peas, defrosted
- 1/4 cup sliced black olives
- For Garnish,
- Hot sauce
- Freshly chopped parsley

Directions:

1. Heat 1 tablespoon olive oil in the rice cooker on a mixed key for 3 minutes. Add onion and bell peppers. Cook until soft, about 7 minutes. Add garlic to the rice cooker and sauté for 1 minute or until fragrant. Add the broth, then fold in smoked paprika, oregano, sea salt, crushed red pepper, black pepper, bay leaf, diced tomatoes with liquid, and rice. Select the Brown Rice key and cook through the cycle.
2. Place the excess oil in the pan and heat. Add chicken thighs and chorizo. Cook until browned and no pink shows in the chicken; about 10 to 12 minutes. Fold cooked chicken and sausage into the rice. Add saffron, peas, and black olives to the rice cooker. Mixed key for 5 minutes to combine flavors. Serve garnished with hot sauce and chopped parsley.

Nutrition: Calories 844 Fat 16.1g Carbohydrates 144g Dietary Fiber 9.3g Protein 36g

Slow Cooked Smoked Spicy Turkey

Preparation Time: 10 minutes

Cooking Time: 9 hours

Servings: 8

Ingredients:

- 1 whole small turkey
- Seasoning Ingredients
- sea salt, to taste
- 1 tsp. liquid smoke flavoring
- 1/2 tsp. cumin
- 1/2 tsp. cayenne pepper
- 1/2 tsp. chili powder

Directions:

1. Set your instapot into slow cooker mode. Crumple 4 pieces of aluminum foil into 4 inch balls on the bottom of your pot. Rinse the meat inside and out with cold water and pat dry. Combine all of the seasoning ingredients. Rub the seasoning ingredients all over the meat. Layer on top of the aluminum foil. Cook on high for an hour and low for 9 hours.

Nutrition: Calories 160 Fat 9g Carbohydrates 1.8g Dietary Fiber 0g Protein 18g

Slow Cooked Smoked Chinese Chili Garlic Chicken

Preparation Time: 10 minutes

Cooking Time: 10 hours

Servings: 4-6

Ingredients:

- 1 whole chicken
- For Seasoning,
- sea salt, to taste
- 1/2 tsp. liquid smoke flavoring
- 1 tsp. Sichuan Peppercorns
- 1 tablespoon Chili Garlic Paste

Directions:

1. Set your instapot into slow cooker mode. Crumple 4 pieces of aluminum foil into 4 inch balls on the bottom of your pot. Rinse the meat inside and out with cold water and pat dry. Combine all of the seasoning ingredients. Rub the seasoning ingredients all over the meat. Layer on top of the aluminum foil. Cook on high for an hour and low for 9 hours.

Nutrition: Calories 255.2 Fat 8.9g Carbohydrates 9.9g Dietary Fiber 1.3g Protein 29.4g

Slow Cooked Honey Chili Garlic Pheasant

Preparation Time: 10 minutes

Cooking Time: 10 hours

Servings: 4

Ingredients:

- 1 whole pheasant
- For Seasoning,
- sea salt, to taste
- 1 tablespoon Sambal Oelek
- 1 tsp. minced cilantro
- 1 tablespoon honey

Directions:

1. Set your instapot into slow cooker mode. Crumple 4 pieces of aluminum foil into 4 inch balls on the bottom of your pot. Rinse the meat inside and out with cold water and pat dry. Combine all of the seasoning ingredients. Rub the seasoning ingredients all over the meat. Layer on top of the aluminum foil. Cook on high for an hour and low for 9 hours.

Nutrition: Calories 144 Fat 3g Protein 20g

Slow Cooked Tunisian Turkey

Preparation Time: 10 minutes

Cooking Time: 10 hours

Servings: 8

Ingredients:

- 1 whole small turkey
- For Seasoning,
- sea salt, to taste
- 1 tablespoon Harissa paste
- 1 tablespoon minced garlic
- 1 tablespoon honey

Directions:

1. Set your instapot into slow cooker mode. Crumple 4 pieces of aluminum foil into 4 inch balls on the bottom of your pot. Rinse the meat inside and out with cold water and pat dry. Combine all of the seasoning ingredients. Rub the seasoning ingredients all over the meat. Layer on top of the aluminum foil. Cook on high for an hour and low for 9 hours.

Nutrition: Calories 455.5 Fat 4.6g Carbohydrates 19.2g Dietary Fiber 3.4g Protein 81.1g

Slow Cooked Smoked Lemongrass Chicken

Preparation Time: 10 minutes

Cooking Time: 10 hours

Servings: 6-8

Ingredients:

- 1 whole chicken
- For Seasoning,
- sea salt, to taste
- 1 tablespoon liquid smoke flavoring
- 3 stalks of lemongrass, coarsely chopped

Directions:

1. Set your instapot into slow cooker mode. Crumple 4 pieces of aluminum foil into 4 inch balls on the bottom of your pot. Rinse the meat inside and out with cold water and pat dry. Combine all of the seasoning ingredients. Rub the seasoning ingredients all over the meat. Layer on top of the aluminum foil. Cook on high for an hour and low for 9 hours.

Nutrition: Calories 9 Fat 0g Carbohydrates 1g Protein 1g

Slow Cooked French Smoked Pheasant

Preparation Time: 10 minutes

Cooking Time: 10 hours

Servings: 4

Ingredients:

- 1 whole pheasant
- For Seasoning,
- sea salt, to taste
- 1 tablespoon liquid smoke flavoring
- 2 tsp. herbs de provence

Directions:

1. Set your instapot into slow cooker mode. Crumple 4 pieces of aluminum foil into 4 inch balls on the bottom of your pot. Rinse the meat inside and out with cold water and pat dry. Combine all of the seasoning ingredients. Rub the seasoning ingredients all over the meat. Layer on top of the aluminum foil. Cook on high for an hour and low for 9 hours.

Nutrition: Calories 256.1 Fat 17.6g Carbohydrates 3.9g Dietary Fiber 0.4g Protein 19.7g

SOUP AND STEWS

Meatball Soup

Preparation Time: 20 minutes

Cooking Time: 40 minutes

Servings: 6

Ingredients:

- 1 egg, beaten
- 1 lb. lean ground beef
- ¾ cup whole-wheat bread crumbs
- cloves garlic, crushed, minced and divided
- teaspoons fresh rosemary, chopped and divided
- Pepper to taste
- 1-tablespoon olive oil
- 1 onion, chopped
- yellow bell peppers, sliced into strips
- carrots, chopped
- cups water
- cups low-sodium beef broth
- ½ cup barley (preferably quick-cooking)

- 15 oz. canned Great Northern beans, rinsed and drained
- cups baby spinach leaves

Directions

1 Preheat your oven to 350 degrees F. Add the egg to a bowl. Stir in the ground beef, breadcrumbs, 2 cloves garlic and 1-teaspoon rosemary. Season it with the pepper. Mix well. Form into balls. Add the meatballs to a baking pan. Bake for 15 minutes. Pour the oil into your Dutch oven. Add the onion, remaining garlic, bell pepper and carrot.

2 Cook for 5 minutes. Pour in the water, broth, remaining rosemary, barley and beans. Bring to a boil. Reduce heat and cover. Simmer for 15 minutes. Add the meatballs, and then simmer for 5 more minutes. Add the spinach before serving.

Nutrition: Calories 301 Fat 10 g Carbohydrates 31 g Protein 25 g

White Chili Soup

Preparation Time: 15 minutes

Cooking Time: 15 minutes

Servings: 6

Ingredients:

- 30 oz. Great Northern beans, rinsed, drained and divided
- 1-tablespoon vegetable oil
- 1 lb. chicken thigh fillet, sliced into smaller pieces
- 1 onion, chopped
- cloves garlic, chopped
- stalks celery, chopped
- Salt to taste
- 1-teaspoon ground cumin
- oz. green chili, chopped
- cups chicken stock
- oz. low-fat cream cheese
- ½ cup fresh cilantro leaves, chopped

Directions:

1 Use a potato masher to mash 1 cup beans in a bowl. Pour the oil into your Dutch oven over high heat. Cook the

chicken until brown on all sides for 3 to 5 minutes. Stir in the onion, garlic, celery, salt and cumin.

2. Cook for 5 minutes. Pour in the mashed beans along with the remaining beans. Add the chili and stock. Bring to a boil. Reduce heat. Cover and simmer for 4 minutes. Stir in the cream cheese. Sprinkle the cilantro on top before serving.

Nutrition: Calories 319 Fat 11.9 g Carbohydrates 29.4 g Fiber 9.4 g Protein 23.1 g

Beef Vegetables

Preparation Time: 20 minutes

Cooking Time: 25 minutes

Servings: 4

Ingredients:

- 1-teaspoon vegetable oil
- 12 oz. beef sirloin steak, fat trimmed and sliced into cubes
- 1 onion, chopped
- cloves garlic, crushed and minced
- 8 oz. fresh mushrooms, sliced
- 28 oz. low-sodium beef stock
- 28 oz. canned diced tomatoes, juice reserved
- 1-tablespoon balsamic vinegar
- ¼ teaspoon fennel seed, crushed
- ½ teaspoon dried Italian seasoning
- Pepper to taste
- 1 yellow bell pepper, chopped
- 1 cup green beans, trimmed and sliced
- cups kale, sliced

Directions:

1. Pour the oil into your Dutch oven over medium high heat. Cook the beef until brown. Transfer the beef to a plate. Add the onion, garlic and mushrooms to the pot. Cook for 6 minutes. Pour in the vinegar. Scrape the browned bits on the pot using a wooden spoon. Add the remaining ingredients except the vegetables. Bring to a boil. Add the bell pepper, green beans and kale. Reduce heat and simmer for 15 minutes.

Nutrition: Calories 209 Fat 5.1 g Carbohydrates 17.1 g Fiber 5.3 g Protein 25 g

Pork Green Chili Stew

Preparation Time: 40 minutes

Cooking Time: 1 hour and 20 minutes

Servings: 8

Ingredients:

- green bell peppers, sliced in half and seeded
- 1 ½ lb. pork shoulder (boneless), fat trimmed and sliced into cubes
- cups onion, chopped
- cloves garlic, crushed and minced
- ¼ cup jalapeño pepper, chopped
- 1 ½ teaspoons fresh oregano leaves, chopped
- Salt to taste
- 1 ½ lb. potatoes, sliced into cubes
- oz. corn kernels
- zucchini, sliced
- ½ cup fresh cilantro leaves, chopped

Directions:

1 Preheat your oven to 425 degrees F. Line your baking pan with foil. Place the bell peppers in the baking pan. Roast for 20 minutes. Let cool and then chop the peppers. Set aside. Add the chopped bell peppers, pork,

onion, garlic, jalapeño pepper, oregano and salt in your Dutch oven. Cover with foil. Bake in the oven at 325 degrees F for 45 minutes. Stir in the potatoes. Cover and bake for another 30 minutes. Add the corn and zucchini. Cover and bake for 15 minutes. Sprinkle with the cilantro before serving.

Nutrition: Calories 269 Fat 6 g Carbohydrates 34 g Protein 22 g

Caribbean Pork Stew

Preparation Time: 10 minutes

Cooking Time: 20 minutes

Servings: 6

Ingredients:

- 15 oz. black beans, rinsed and drained
- cups water
- 15 oz. canned beef broth
- 12 oz. lean pork, sliced into strips
- 1 tablespoon fresh ginger, grated
- 1 cup tomatoes, chopped
- cups stir fry vegetables
- plantains, sliced into cubes
- ¼-teaspoon red pepper flakes
- 1-teaspoon ground cumin
- Salt to taste
- cups brown rice, cooked

Directions:

1 Add the black beans to your Dutch oven. Pour in the water and broth. Bring to a boil. Stir in the rest of the ingredients except the rice. Reduce heat and simmer for 10 minutes. Serve the pork stew with the rice.

Nutrition: Calories 401 Fat 6.6 g Carbohydrates 64.5 g Protein 25.3 g

Southern Stew

Preparation Time: 40 minutes

Cooking Time: 55 minutes

Servings: 8

Ingredients:

- 1-tablespoon vegetable oil
- 1 onion, diced
- stalks celery, chopped
- carrots, sliced thinly
- Salt and pepper to taste
- ½ teaspoon dried thyme
- ¼-teaspoon red pepper flakes
- cloves garlic, chopped
- tablespoons tomato paste
- cups chicken stock (unsalted)
- 15 oz. canned diced tomatoes
- 1 bay leaf
- 1 lb. turkey thighs and drumsticks, smoked
- 1 lb. potatoes, sliced
- cups corn kernels
- cups okra, sliced
- cups lima beans

- tablespoons brown sugar
- tablespoons cider vinegar
- ⅓ cup Worcestershire sauce

Directions:

1 Pour the oil into your Dutch oven over medium high heat. Cook the onion, celery, carrot, salt and pepper for 3 minutes. Stir in the thyme, pepper flakes and garlic. Cook while stirring for 1 to 2 minutes. Stir in the tomato paste and cook for 1 minute. Pour in the chicken stock and tomatoes. Add the bay leaf. Bring to a boil over high heat. Add the turkey, potatoes, corn, okra and lima beans. Bring to a boil. Reduce heat.

2 Simmer for 20 minutes. Season the dish with the brown sugar, vinegar, salt and Worcestershire sauce. Simmer for 10 minutes. Place the turkey on a cutting board. Chop the turkey meat. Simmer the stew for 10 more minutes. Put the chopped turkey back to the stew. Simmer for 2 more minutes before serving.

Nutrition: Calories 305 Fat 5.9 g Carbohydrates 43.5 g Protein 23.2 g

VEGETABLES

Frittata with Spinach and Meat

Preparation Time: 10 minutes

Cooking Time: 20 minutes

Servings: 2

Ingredients

- oz ground turkey
- oz of spinach leaves
- 1/3 tsp minced garlic
- 1/3 tsp coconut oil
- eggs
- Seasoning:
- 1/3 tsp salt
- ¼ tsp ground black pepper

Directions:

1 Turn on the oven, then set it to 400 degrees F, and let it preheat.

2. Meanwhile, take a skillet pan, place it over medium heat, add spinach and cook for 3 to 5 minutes until spinach leaves have wilted, remove the pan from heat.
3. Take a small heatproof skillet pan, place it over medium heat, add ground turkey and cook for 5 minutes until thoroughly cooked.
4. Then add spinach, season with salt and black pepper, stir well, then remove the pan from heat and spread the mixture evenly in the pan.
5. Crack eggs in a bowl, season with salt and black pepper, then pour this mixture over spinach mixture in the pan and bake for 10 to 15 minutes until frittata has thoroughly cooked and the top is golden brown.
6. When done, let frittata rest in the pan for 5 minutes, then cut it into slices and serve.

Nutrition: 166 Calories 13 g Fats 10 g Protein 0.5 g Net Carb 0.5 g Fiber

Avocado Egg Boat with Cheddar

Preparation Time: 5 minutes

Cooking Time: 15 minutes

Servings: 2

Ingredients

- 1 avocado, halved, pitted
- eggs
- tbsp chopped bacon
- tbsp shredded cheddar cheese
- Seasoning:
- 1/8 tsp salt
- 1/8 tsp ground black pepper

Directions:

1. Turn on the oven, then set it to 400 degrees F and let it preheat.
2. Meanwhile, prepare avocado and for this, cut it into half lengthwise and then remove the pit.
3. Scoop out some of the flesh from the center, crack an egg into each half, then sprinkle with bacon and season with salt and black pepper.

4. Sprinkle cheese over egg and avocado and then bake for 10 to 15 minutes or until the yolk has cooked to desired level. Serve.

Nutrition: 263.5 Calories 21.4 g Fats 12 g Protein 1.3 g Net Carb 4.6 g Fiber

Cauliflower Fritters

Preparation Time: 5 minutes

Cooking Time: 8 minutes

Servings: 2

Ingredients

- ½ cup cauliflower florets
- tbsp shredded cheddar cheese
- ½ of egg
- 1 tbsp avocado oil
- Seasoning:
- ¼ tsp salt
- 1/8 tsp ground black pepper

Directions:

1. Take a food processor, add cauliflower florets in it, then pulse them until finely chopped and tip the florets into a heatproof bowl.
2. Cover the bowl with a plastic wrap, pork holes by using a fork and then microwave for 2 minutes or until just tender.
3. Then add remaining ingredients except for oil and stir well until incorporated and cheese has melted.

4. Take a skillet pan, place it over medium heat, add oil and when hot, drop in ¼ of the batter, shape it into patties and cook for 3 minutes per side until crispy and browned.
5. Serve.

Nutrition: 92 Calories 7.2 g Fats 4.6 g Protein 2 g Net Carb 1.3 g Fiber

Brussel Sprouts Bacon Breakfast Hash

Preparation Time: 5 minutes

Cooking Time: 25 minutes

Servings: 2

Ingredients

- oz Brussel sprouts, sliced
- slices of bacon, chopped
- ½ tsp minced garlic
- ¾ tbsp apple cider vinegar
- eggs

Directions:

1 Place a skillet pan over medium heat and when hot, add bacon and cook for 5 to 7 minutes until crispy.

2 Transfer bacon to a plate, add garlic and cook for 30 seconds until fragrant.

3 Then add Brussel sprouts, stir in vinegar and cook for 5 minutes until tender.

4 Return bacon into the pan, cook for 5 minutes until sprouts are golden brown, then create a well in the pan and cracks the egg in it.

5 Cook the eggs for 3 to 5 minutes until cooked to the desired level and then serve immediately.

Nutrition: 134.5 Calories 8.2 g Fats 10.8 g Protein 2.8 g Net Carb 1.6 g Fiber

Cauliflower and Bacon Hash

Preparation Time: 5 minutes

Cooking Time: 15 minutes

Servings: 2

Ingredients

- ½ cup chopped cauliflower florets
- slices of bacon, diced
- ¼ tsp paprika
- 1 tbsp avocado oil
- Seasoning:
- 1/3 tsp salt
- 1/8 tsp ground black pepper
- 1 ½ tbsp water

Directions:

1 Take a skillet pan, place it over medium-high heat, add bacon, and cook for 3 to 5 minutes until crispy. Transfer bacon to a plate, then add cauliflower into the pan and cook for 3 minutes until golden.

2. Season with salt, black pepper, and paprika, drizzle with water, and cook for 3 to 5 minutes until cauliflower has softened. Chop the bacon, add it into the pan, stir well, cook for 2 minutes and then remove the pan from heat. Serve.

Nutrition: 211.5 Calories 18.6 g Fats 9 g Protein 1.3 g Net Carb 0.3 g Fiber

Greens and Orange Salad

Preparation Time: 15 minutes

Cooking Time: 0 minute

Servings: 4

Ingredients:

- 1 avocado, pitted, peeled and chopped
- cups mixed salad greens
- tablespoons pine nuts, toasted
- figs, cut into quarters
- ¾ cup pomegranate seeds
- oranges, peeled and cut into segments
- ¼ cup extra virgin olive oil
- 1 tablespoon lemon juice
- tablespoons orange juice
- tablespoons white wine vinegar

- 1 teaspoon orange zest
- A pinch of sea salt
- Black pepper to taste

Directions:

1. In a salad bowl, mix greens with avocado, figs, oranges, pine nuts and pomegranate seeds. In another bowl, mix orange juice with lemon juice, olive oil, orange zest, vinegar, a pinch of sea salt and pepper to taste and whisk well.
2. Pour this over salad, toss to coat and serve.

Nutrition: 427 calories 26g fat 8.8g fiber

SNACK AND DESSERTS

Blueberry Cheesecake Stuffed French Toast

Preparation Time: 10 minutes

Cooking Time: 5 minutes

Serving: 4

Ingredients:

- 1 cup blueberries
- tablespoons sugar
- ½ cup water
- 1 (8-ounce) package cream cheese, softened
- ½ cup powdered sugar
- large eggs
- ½ cup half-and-half
- 1 teaspoon vanilla extract
- ½ teaspoon ground cinnamon
- 1 loaf of sliced French bread
- Butter for greasing skillet
- Whipped topping
- Maple syrup

Directions:

1. In a small skillet over medium-high heat, combine blueberries with sugar and ½ cup water and bring to boil. Reduce heat to low and simmer for 10 minutes. Puree blueberry sauce in a food processor with cream cheese and powdered sugar. Allow to cool for 10 minutes.
2. In a bowl whisk together eggs, half-and-half, vanilla, and cinnamon. Slice bread into 1-inch thick slices, with a slit halfway through the center of each piece. Using a spoon, stuff opening in bread with blueberry cheesecake filling.
3. Soak each side of a slice of bread in egg mixture. Grease skillet with butter. Toast bread for 1 to 2 minutes on each side in a large skillet over medium heat. Top with whipped topping and maple syrup.

Nutrition: 118 calories 1g fiber 12g fats

Dark Chocolate Scones

Preparation Time: 10 minutes

Cooking Time: 15 minutes

Serving: 8

Ingredients:

- cups all-purpose flour
- ¼ cup firmly packed light brown sugar
- teaspoons baking powder
- teaspoons ground cinnamon
- ½ teaspoon salt
- tablespoons butter, cut into half-inch cubes
- ⅔ cup milk, divided
- 1 cup dark chocolate chunks
- Turbinado sugar

Directions:

1 Preheat oven to 375 degrees. In the bowl of an electric mixer combine flour, brown sugar, baking powder, cinnamon, and salt on low speed for 10 seconds. Add butter to bowl, continuing to mix until butter is evenly distributed in small crumbs.

2. Slowly pour milk into flour mixture and mix until incorporated, reserving about 1 tablespoon of milk. Fold chocolate chunks into dough.
3. Empty dough onto a flat surface and fold dough in half once vertically and horizontally to evenly incorporate chocolate. Roll dough into a 1-inch thick rectangle and transfer to parchment paper–lined baking sheet.
4. Spread the reserved 1 tablespoon of milk over top of dough and sprinkle with turbinado sugar. Bake for 17 to 19 minutes. Allow to cool for 5 minutes before slicing into 8 triangles.

Nutrition: 114 calories 2g fiber 22g carbs

Pumpkin and Pecan Baked Oatmeal

Preparation Time: 15 minutes

Cooking Time: 5 minutes

Serving: 6

Ingredients:

- cups quick-cooking oats
- 1 cup firmly packed light brown sugar
- 1 teaspoon baking powder
- 1 teaspoon ground cinnamon
- ½ teaspoon ground nutmeg
- ½ teaspoon salt
- ½ cup pumpkin puree
- ¾ cup evaporated milk
- 1 teaspoon vanilla extract
- 1 large egg
- ½ cup chocolate chips
- ¼ cup pecans

Directions:

1 Preheat oven to 350 degrees. In a large bowl stir together oats, brown sugar, baking powder, cinnamon, nutmeg, and salt. In a separate bowl mix pumpkin puree, evaporated milk, vanilla, and egg.

2 Combine pumpkin puree mixture with oat mixture. Fold in chocolate chips. Transfer batter to a greased 9 × 9-inch baking dish. Top with pecans. Bake for 35 minutes.

Nutrition: 120 calories 21g carbs 3g protein

Herbed Mini Quiches

Preparation Time: 10 minutes

Cooking Time: 20 minutes

Serving: 36

Ingredients:

- ounces butter crackers
- tablespoons butter, melted
- 1 large egg white
- ¾ cup grated Parmesan cheese
- (8-ounce) packages cream cheese
- ¼ teaspoon salt
- ¼ teaspoon black pepper
- 1 teaspoon chopped fresh parsley
- ¼ teaspoon dried dill
- large eggs
- ½ teaspoon lemon juice
- 1 teaspoon chopped chives

Directions:

1. Preheat oven to 350 degrees. In a food processor pulse together crackers, butter, egg white, and ¼ cup Parmesan cheese. Press crumbs into bottom of cups of mini muffin pan. Bake crust for 6 to 8 minutes, until lightly brown.
2. In the food processor combine cream cheese, salt, pepper, ½ cup Parmesan, parsley, dill, eggs, and lemon juice. Fold in chives and pour batter onto crusts. Bake for 13 to 15 minutes. Top with additional parsley.

Nutrition: 113 calories 20g carbs 1g fiber

White Chocolate French Toast Kabobs

Preparation Time: 10 minutes

Cooking Time: 10 minutes

Serving: 4

Ingredients:

- ¾ cup half-and-half
- 1 teaspoon vanilla extract
- tablespoons butter
- tablespoons firmly packed light brown sugar
- ½ teaspoon ground cinnamon
- ¼ teaspoon salt
- ⅔ cup white chocolate chips
- large eggs
- 1 loaf of sliced French bread
- Butter for greasing skillet
- cups blackberries
- peaches, sliced
- Maple syrup

Directions:

1 In a medium saucepan over low heat stir half-and-half, vanilla, butter, brown sugar, cinnamon, salt, and white chocolate until melted. Allow to cool.

2. In a bowl whisk eggs and incorporate into half-and-half mixture.
3. Soak each side of a slice of bread in egg mixture. Grease skillet with butter. Toast bread for 1 to 2 minutes on each side in a large skillet over medium heat. Repeat with remaining slices.
4. Slice French toast into 1-inch cubes. Assemble kabobs on skewers with French toast pieces, blackberries, and peaches. Drizzle with maple syrup.

Nutrition: 116 calories 11g fats 3g fiber

Maple Sweet Potato Hash Browns

Preparation Time: 5 minutes

Cooking Time: 15 minutes

Serving: 4

Ingredients:

- cups water
- sweet potatoes, cubed
- 1-pound bacon
- ½ yellow onion, diced
- 1 teaspoon garlic powder
- ½ teaspoon red pepper flakes
- Salt to taste
- Black pepper to taste
- large eggs, fried
- Maple syrup

Directions:

1 Bring a large pot of 8 cups water to boil over high heat. Add potatoes and reduce heat to medium. Cook for 10 minutes.

2 Heat reserved bacon fat in a large skillet over medium-high heat and then add the potatoes and the onion. Fry until the potatoes are crispy, about 10 to 12 minutes. Remove from heat and fold in cooked bacon. Season with garlic powder, red pepper flakes, salt, and pepper.

3 Top with fried eggs and drizzle with maple syrup.

Nutrition: 120 calories 24g carbs 4g protein

Vegan Kit Kat

Preparation Time: 10 minutes

Cooking Time: 3 minutes

Serving: 3

Ingredients

- 1 Cup Semi-Sweet Chocolate Chips
- 1 Tablespoon Coconut Oil
- 12 Vanilla or Chocolate Vegan Wafers

Directions:

1 Melt together chocolate chips and coconut oil over a double boiler or in a microwave. Dip wafers into the chocolate mixture and set on parchment paper. Use a pair of tongs if needed. Allow the chocolate to set. Enjoy!

Nutrition: 146 Calories 13.3g Carbohydrates 1.3g Proteins

Protein Donuts

Preparation Time: 15 minutes

Cooking Time: 15 minutes

Serving: 3

Ingredients

- Tablespoons Coconut Flour
- Tablespoons Non-Dairy Milk
- 1 Tablespoon Peanut Butter
- 1 Flax Egg
- 1/2 Banana

Directions:

1 Combine together all the ingredients and mix well. Line donut pans with some parchment paper. Pour in the mixture. Bake for 10 minutes at 350 degrees.

2 Allow to cool a little before popping out. Drizzle with a chocolate sauce or glaze of choice.

Nutrition 95 Calories 9.1g Carbohydrates 2.8g Proteins

Coconut Cream Cake

Preparation Time: 30 minutes

Cooking Time: 30-35 minutes

Servings: 8-12

Ingredients:

- cups all-purpose flour
- 2/3 cups sugar
- large eggs
- 1 package frozen flaked coconut (6 ounces)
- 1 ½ cup butter, softened
- 1 teaspoon vanilla extract
- ½ teaspoon salt
- 1 cup milk
- 1 teaspoon baking powder
- 1 cup coconut shavings
- teaspoon baking powder
- Coconut Filling:
- ¼ cup powdered sugar
- cups whipping cream
- ½ cup coconut flakes
- 1 teaspoon coconut extract
- 1 teaspoon vanilla extract

Directions:

1 Preheat the oven to 400°F. Beat the flour, sugar, butter, milk, baking powder, and salt together at medium speed with an electric mixer until well blended. Add the extracts and blend well. Gradually start adding the eggs, one at a time, beating until all the ingredients are blended. Stir in the flaked coconut, and pour the batter in to 4 individual cake pans.

2 Bake the cakes for 20 minutes, and then cool on wire racks 10 minutes before removing them from the pans. Reduce the oven temperature to 350°F and bake the coconut shavings in a single layer in a shallow pan, for 10 minutes or until toasted, stirring occasionally. Set the toasted coconut aside. Beat whipping cream on high speed until foamy, and slowly add the coconut and vanilla extracts, coconut flakes and powdered sugar, beating the mixture until soft peaks start to foam.

3 When the cakes have cooled, prepare the coconut filling and spread it between the layers. Spread the remaining frosting on the top and sides of the cake, and carefully press toasted coconut into the frosting. Keep chilled until ready to serve.

Nutrition: Calories: 385 Fat: 27.6g Fiber: 1.5g Carbs: 65g Protein: 1g

Strawberry Shortcake

Preparation Time: 30 minutes

Cooking Time: 25-30minutes

Servings: 8-12

Ingredients:

- pounds fresh strawberries, hulled and quartered
- ¾ cup sugar, divided
- ¾ cup cold butter
- large eggs
- 1 cup whipping cream
- ¼ teaspoon almond extract
- 1 container sour cream (8 ounces)
- 1 teaspoon vanilla extract
- teaspoon baking powder
- ¾ cups all-purpose flour
- tablespoons sugar

Directions:

1 Combine the strawberries, ½ cup sugar, and almond extract. Cover the mixture and allow it to rest for 10 minutes. At a medium speed, beat the whipping cream with an electric mixture until foamy. Slowly add 2 tablespoons of sugar, beating until soft peaks start to

form. Cover the mixture and keep refrigerated until ready to use.

2 Preheat the oven to 450°F. Combine the flour, remaining ¼ cup sugar and baking powder in a large bowl. Cut the butter into the flour mixture with pastry blender until crumbly.

3 In another bowl, whisk together sour cream, eggs, and vanilla until well blended, then add to the flour mixture and stir until all the dry ingredients are moistened. Drop dough by lightly greased ⅓ cupful onto a lightly greased baking sheet, and bake for 12 to 15 minutes until golden.

4 Cut the shortcakes in half horizontally, and spoon ½ cup of the berry mixture and scoop it on the bottom of the short cake, top with a tablespoon of whipped cream, cover the top and serve with the remaining whipped cream.

Nutrition: Calories: 415 Fat: 19.5g Fiber: 1.6g Carbs: 45.9g Protein: 3g

LOVE

CPSIA information can be obtained
at www.ICGtesting.com
Printed in the USA
BVHW062326220321
603180BV00003B/547